THE PHYSICIST AT THE MALL

For Leigh —
With all good wishes
for your writing —

Janet

6·11·98
Bogue Sound

THE PHYSICIST AT THE MALL

JANET HOLMES

Janet Holmes (signature)

1993 Anhinga Prize for Poetry
Our Tenth Anniversary Selection
Joy Harjo, Judge

ANHINGA
PRESS

TALLAHASSEE, FLORIDA
1 9 9 3

Library of Congress Cataloging in Publication Data
Holmes, Janet
The Physicist at the Mall

(The Anhinga Prize for Poetry, 1993)
I. Title II. Series: Anhinga Poetry Prize Series
Library of Congress Catalog Card Number
ISBN: 0-938078-37-2

Printed in the United States of America
First Edition: January 1994

Cover Art and Design by David Wilder
Book Design and Production by Donna J. Long

Anhinga Press thanks the following for their help in selecting
this manuscript from over 300 entries: Melanie Abrahms,
Frances Brock, Tom Heise, Ray McDaniel, Donna Parks,
Catherine Reid, John E. Simpson, Michael Trammel,
Rex West, Toni Whitfield

Anhinga Press, Inc. is a nonprofit corporation staffed by
volunteers and dedicated wholly to the publication and
appreciation of fine poetry.

Author's acknowledgements appear on page 60.

Para Luisito Lujan, con cariño

CONTENTS

Pathetic Fallacy

The narrow highways keep us
tenuously tied, like the satin straps
of last night's fancy dress
undoing themselves at my shoulder. They aren't
the articulate shortcuts of cities, or routes of affection
urgent as new arroyos in floodtime,
but cliffhangers, hairpin curves, trick loops,
and they go on for miles. I can't keep my eye on the road
as I leave you. It's beautiful:
a cloud band wraps the mountains,
a stole of cotton catching the day's last gold,
like the halo wound round the head
of a sitting girl in a small-town beauty shop.
"With this," the hairdresser said,
pinning it all in place, "the stuff won't burn out
your eyes . . ." while the lotion, caustic, ran down
the tight coils of hair to my scalp
and soaked the cotton rope. It didn't blind me,
so I could be married the next day in curls
all the way to my shoulders, to learn that *permanent*
means temporary, but longer.
It takes me hours, well through the winding pass
and almost home, to see the clouds
as clouds again. A bunch to one side
settles low in a valley, while from those ahead
rain falls without reaching earth:
virga, that's called, streaks of white water
dead in the air—unconsummated rain,
you might say. I don't let nature speak to me
in cumuli assuming monstrous shapes;
I don't let the weather make me moody.
No, I drove away from you knowing nothing's
writ large on the world's plain face
but this: water gathers itself
out of air, into clouds;
gathers itself, grows heavy, falls,
and waits to gather again.

THE PATTERN

Imperfect memory: snowflakes
creating themselves in their own image
never get it exactly right.
So what you end up with are all these
pleasant approximations: this many points,
that much filigree betwixt,
but no matched pairs. The same
with leaves, their veins and serrate edges.
The same with smoke: the wisps
from twenty identical
votive candles at the shrine
are not identical; they remember only
a general way of rising, curling,
fading. What do you want?
Patterns that make you utter
surprise—nonlinear
plots, fractal
repetitions, Mandelbrot sets,
a template
in the chaotic
penetralia. A winter-white
landscape, its perfect
peace. Woodfires
coiling smoke up the chimney
this year, as in all the others.
In the spring, the leaves coming out
fleshy and soft on the branches
as if on cue, no two alike. You want
a miracle that knows its place: when to be
explicable, and when (your daughter
first stretching her mouth into a grin
you recognize as yours)
an utter surprise.

THE MILKY WAY

The first Mary was stolen, so now Our Lady
prays behind bars outside the Nambé Church, her *nicho*
lit like a small stadium. The church's hill
affords a view of the mountains appropriately scenic,
but I took you behind it to look straight up in darkness
at August's meteors, shielding the Virgin's klieg
with adobe.
            Well, citydweller, you weren't prepared
for an unlit sky in this bare country, no streetlights
reflecting up to clouds, a clear space
so filled up with stars
it seemed theoretical: what *might* exist out there
if we could see—
            you reminded me
of myself, sixth grade, learning constellations
with Randy Konigsberg out on my front lawn,
California beneath our backs, head to head,
the astrochart passing between us. Even that young,
my thoughts slid down to where I was (*what if
he and I . . .*)
            as, behind the church, neck craned back,
what if, I thought again . . .
            as if the universe,
brought home as more than bright small points
attractively arranged, forced people closer together
for something like protection, to keep them
from flying off the planet toward something
with more pull. I wanted to hold on,
                        and you
seemed so much more concrete
than anything else—mudwalled church, stone saint,
earth—
            The Milky Way stretched over us like a sea,
and everywhere the random stars made pictures,
heroes and bears that look (on a chart) like
geometric proofs
            and (in the sky) like fireflies,

meteors shooting through trying to prove
there's life out there, there's movement,
though you can tell that you're alone,
and I didn't reach out, but waited to fall in . . .

CHARLESTON

Let's pick up then, Donna, from the New York summer
you moved in with that soap-opera actor
and I went to that college town with my husband
to finish our sorry partnership.
I was learning to use a computer when I finally
left him and moved in with three girl students
to share a house where one room was all mine.
Every day I went out with new plans: to go back to the city,
to be friends with men. When you
went through that loneliness, you'd say
even the man behind the counter at Balducci's
looks good to me now. But I saw each
as worth a little fear still, to wit:
that day my husband came to the office
and threw the cigarette machine across the hall
because I was talking with a guy he didn't like.
It took three of us to move the damned thing
back, and a long time before I talked
to anybody. One day someone told me I'd gotten
too quiet and needed to get away.
Oh, I told him, can't do it, I'm broke.
We'll go to Charleston, he said, as if
we knew each other. It's romantic—peaceful—
and no one here would know where you were.
Well, we laughed. And if I sat at my terminal
he'd send that word to my screen: *Charleston!*
like a promise. We started to be in love
over the idea of a rescuing place. I thought
it made sense, moving and changing partners
in order to change my life. And it worked
for a while. We traveled from Key West
to the Arctic, and I learned about seasons
and geography, the camouflage of innocent questions,
how to pull up a tent, bury things with woodfire ashes
and drive away. It's true
we never went exactly to Charleston. I think of it—
nebulous, perfect, a Southern town that waits

for my most desperate time with its mansions and flora
white as bridal lace. I think of you, Donna,
of Balducci's, of the man I came here with,
who's gone now, of the miles I marked off,
and I don't feel I need Charleston just yet.
But I want it there: white and green, full of damp heat,
waiting for me, its streets opened like arms,
waiting as people never can, or won't.

Muscle Memory

The dancer's legs scallop the air:
each night for the run of the season
the same silhouette.

Her muscles remember the *tour jété,*
entrechats quatre, entrechats six;
many things the dancer believes are automatic,

as the athlete knows the feel of a goal
almost before his hands launch the ball.

The pianist runs through her oldest concerto
dreaming of water, or love, carrying
the melody forward without thought.

Somatic wisdom: ligaments,
tendons, and pulp.
We say *practice makes perfect,*

which is why the years and distance
hardly matter: my body
slides into place with yours so calmly

that we might have been together all this time.

CHEZ PERSEPHONE

I like it here. You might as well
learn to love your winters—

each time I go to you
more reluctant, riding with zebras

and leopards, that pageant of spangles.
You make elaborate fusses; I stand around

in garlands.
We can't go on like this.

I get this one big party, then months
alone, with my mother.

Here, I'm not responsible for
the clouds, the people bring

gifts of blue glass
when they visit, there's no

paperwork. A house of slate
and satin!

Thinking of you
in all that whiteness, the wet

branches, the long, long nights,
I don't really want

the earth again: there's
no need for sacrifices,

friends. Oh I could stand
some minor worship

in this underworld marriage—
but standard celebrations, adoration

of millions, a virtual
fan club of mortals

reminds me of so much snow.
Spring doesn't last, and was

too much like heaven, anyway.

OTHER LONGEVITIES

If, like snakes or reptiles, we grew with years,
then imagine the huge elderly, slowed
with age and bulk, frequenting
delicatessens, libraries; crowding
laundromats; taking whole booths to themselves
in family restaurants. The ample bodies
of the long-married, ambling their constitutionals.
The memories, all of smaller times.
Regardless of our wisdom or kindness, faith
or virtue, regardless of our capacity
for loneliness or independence, we would each grow
larger and more splendid,
and, lying down, would dream again and again
of childhood—the narrow long road back
to the vanishing point—each new dream
permitting another to be forgotten.

Before the Parade

A few blocks north, a few avenues over
from our too-dark, too-small place, they lay out
limp monsters: giant dog, giant frog, a moose.
It's Thanksgiving eve; so, ceremoniously,
we walk uptown to watch the trucks, the men with rope,
the bustling people in coveralls, and in among them
the uncountable kids with their skateboards and music.
You work part-time at the store, and hate it. Today

a man, evenly grayed with dust, as if to match
himself to his crosshatched scalp, held you with steady eyes
while his body wavered. "Listen," he said.
"I'm going to tell you something that will *amaze* you."
He punched the fourth button of your uniform shirt
with his twisted finger, and you stood helpless, waiting,
until he continued: "*I* was in the *first-ever*
Macy's Thanksgiving parade." In your voice,

as you told the story, sang all the disappointment
of a squandered visit from the oracle, a certain
harsh pity for his easy wonder.
We thought the spectacle of preparation
would fix your bad feeling, and with
our friend, the man she loves, and his two children, wander
purposefully in the chaos, pretending to do this
just for his children's amusement. The girl is six

and mixes excitedly in the commotion, but the boy,
fourteen, won't walk with us—embarrassed, we imagine,
in the usual teenage way. His father and our friend
are awkward around him. Later, he disappears.
You and I weave through the crowd, looking
away from each other, away from our linked arms,
as if for the tonic all this was going to supply.
I can picture us coming back one day and, with something

like astonishment, witnessing
to some nearly featureless kid: *Listen,*
we were young and married, and, for a time,
were happy. In the street
the enormous balloons go on for a block, flattened
and ready. The boy shows up again,
sullen and still apart, but his sister
runs back and forth among us, calling

"I wish it was tomorrow now! I want it to be
tomorrow," when what we have at our feet
will be airborne, vanishing, gone.

HIBISCUS

Red, silky, lavish, it still
must have been an easy plant to grow—
it was everywhere at the Florida house, while
the ferns died, the aloes died, the grass
yellowed with strange diseases,
and the vines along the fence
turned their passion flowers to face
the neighbors. At pruning time
my mother struggled cutting
her one successful plant until my brother,
Allen, took over the job. From Allen
I learned to catch a feeding bee
in a hibiscus bloom, pulling all the petals
over it, plucking, and dropping the flowerhead
into the ready jar. Or you could shake
the red pod to make it buzz, holding it
next to a person's ear like a satin rattle.
Allen did that, without regard
for angry insects, his sister,
or the brown velvet bruises where our fingers
pinched the petals;
but afterward gave me, to guard,
the mayonnaise jar filled with hibiscus
gently unfolding with bees, opening
as if for the first time, proclaiming
that particular red
with a series of tiny explosions against the glass,
and a constant hum.

TALL DARK MAN ASLEEP ON A BENCH

No one wakes him
as if the neighborhood had bargained to guard him
in return for his daily patrol—a swagger,
his high head lifted, right hand busy with a cigarette
held as carefully as Astaire holds his cane. I heard
someone call him Phil once; it's right
for him, sort of haughty: royalty
living in reduced circumstances.
Bald in the cold, he squats by the Ansonia,
telling us hello, making a church
with his fingers;

     or sits on the curb at the grocer's
eating bananas with the kids. He picks paper clutter
out of the streets with girlish delicacy, fills
his large hands, then leaves the heap
in the back seat of someone's car.

       And he likes
to give money away. I was at the counter
in the Burger Joint when he came in, all tall shadow,
and announced, "I have a nickel someone can have!"
leaving it, finally, next to the plate
of a pale and well-wrapped girl, whose mother
(after he'd left, and we'd laughed, relieved he'd done
nothing threatening) slapped her child's hand and said
coins were dirty. Today

when he reached for my arm and told me it was dangerous,
running like that across Broadway in high heels—
I could catch my foot on something—it didn't seem right
to pull away. He had so much
conviction. He seemed like the tall dark man
I'd been warned about in horoscopes,
in fortune cookies, the one
who gives advice nobody heeds, the one
with the tragic past. Tomorrow he'll be
just himself again, maybe named Phil; but today,
without knowing what questions I had,
I stopped, and let him talk.

THE PHYSICIST AT THE MALL

He grows daily more hesitant, having made doubt
his particular art. A woman in the mall
sells plants in pots sudden with color,
clay proclamations definite and primary,
of mock ethnicity, though she—
an unknown with slender hands,
her smile a tilde of approximation—
is something authentic. The physicist
surrenders himself to unknowns,
as if there were a coefficient
of fascination, one that decreased
with acquaintance, but began
infinitely high (obsession
being natural to researchers) . . .

She toys with her pendant, rose quartz,
wagging it along its silver chain
absently, to boredom's time signature.
Yes, there was somebody in his past,
if you must know, though unlike this
teenaged retailer;
an almost featureless memory now,
with whom he described a curve

of e to the minus t,
which he considers a function
of pure sadness:
infinitely approaching, never equal
to, zero; never the Boolean go or no-go
of pregnancy, say, or a final
slap in the face, or a goodbye.
The rose quartz crystal signifies

a new superstition, he understands,
remembering astrology fondly, his old
frustrating nemesis:

he was about this salesgirl's age then,
arguing bitterly
that even if there *were* truth
in the fabulous predictions,
how could he put his trust there

knowing the common Zodiac
lagged a full constellation in the cycle
of twenty-six thousand years—
the sun not in Virgo now, but Leo,
as the Tropic of Cancer is, more accurately,
Tropic of Gemini? Facts,
which ought to out-power
the thaumaturgy of name and habit

but do not. The Lord God created
heaven and earth in six days, and rested
on Sunday. (For example.) Turn your face
to the night sky, he'd said,
and examine the stars: *calculate*
where the sun is or isn't!
(This, before he learned his air
of professional reservation, "Yes,

but then again, no . . .")
The astrologist had been a girlfriend,
but he'd gone off trembling, having muttered
"Beauty times brains is a constant,"
that lovely, all-insulting
undergraduate witticism, just loud enough
to know she'd heard him.
Last spring, in this same mall,

he was cajoled by some colleagues
into letting a pretty charlatan snap
a ten-buck New Age Polaroid
that purported to show his aura.

Ridiculous—yet he so liked the picture
(the skeptic in his reddish-purple halo)
that he kept it in his office
as a data point, reference

to the uncertain times he lives in;
one's private doubts are excusable . . .
and private. We're human, with human
requirements: clothing, footwear,
decorative plants, all the commerce
of a mall. The physicist
re-orbits the girl in her booth, the rose-quartz
pendant. He one time made a study

of the stress factors
inherent in the engineering
of a strapless dress. Now that,
that is truth: even today, he carries
all the calculations in his head.

Listener in the Stars

I.   Portrait of a Man in Costume

In the four a.m. light, with the streetlight,
the moon, and the white
cheap curtains radiant from them both,
my father is sitting, singing tunelessly
a sentimental song from the twenties,
and drinking bourbon—or he will drink,
soon, from the water-stained glass.
He can make out the gleam of its upper rim,
the cool amber surface
moonlit . . .
                    It is enough to see only this
at this hour
(white reflection on the still liquid)
and enough to hear the melody
even the singer seems barely to recognize
follow the light out to its sources,
as if it sought a listener in the stars

or, farther, the other emptiness
not in this room.

II.   Performance Under Lights

How skillful the pirouette
of the man who, inexplicable,
dances at the horizon alone.
Can't hear his footfalls from here.
He balances mid-air.

How gracefully his arm
beckons to the audience, we
who simply applaud.
None joins him. None
is worthy! We call *encore!*

. . . and yet do not recall
the dance, the dancer's face,
his flashing body, can't
remember shapes or patterns.
But know it happened.

III. A Photo

Here I am one year old, and he, fifty-five. Even then
the road between us was as sparsely traveled
as those between Wisconsin farmtowns: see
how gingerly he holds me. For reporters, children are soon
old news, when men may or may not have murdered
their wives, women their millionaire husbands, and each day
brings a blank page large as the screen of the mind.
Later, I'd wait for the slam and echo
of the oak front door after midnight: the paper in bed,
me out of mine and already journeying farther
than downstairs
                         to the lit kitchen, the interrupted
nightly recitation of the day . . .

IV. Preparation

After retirement, he still fell asleep
about when the morning editions came out
and rode the night through debating, half-audibly,
some old opponent, or else himself.
My brother and I sneaked home, late,
from separate adventures—and as for Dad,
his eyes failed; he moved by shuffling,
stroking ahead with a hand that trembled
winglike, all light bones.
At seventy-five, at my wedding,
he must have thought I'd be embarrassed
if he were slow, so instead
                         he raced me down the aisle;
the organist, into the first few bars
of the processional,
continued to play, and my father patted my arm—
a satisfied, soft gesture—
while we waited the music out.

V.   After the Death

The sheets still held
his smell of soap and shaving cream

and his last vague shape,
the shadow of his weight.

To strip them
was to say goodbye more finally

than later, over the box.
I bundled them in my arms

as, kneeling, you might reach out
to three or four small children

and hug them all at once,
and not release them

to the randomly hurtful world
with any haste.

The Love of the Flesh

Reality is not limited to the tactile:
still, we touch our own faces, as if by the slide
of fingers over cheekbones, eyelids, lips,

we can check that we are not dreaming. This is
the life of the body, the life of gesture,

tangible, a palm against the skin.
When I put my hand to your face it becomes a caress,
but here, against my own, it is disbelief
or wonder.

The questions are hard, as when medieval scholars
divvied up the body in debate
as to where the soul hung its ephemeral hat—

and those who plumped for the heart laboring its fenced-in field
shouted down those others who felt God's messages
precisely in the pit of the stomach,

while the ancients reasoned *the brain, the unromantic brain*,
and virtually every organ had its champion . . .

Their filigree of argument confounds me
just as, then,
the suddenness of love left me dazed:

for days they had to call me twice
to get a single answer—I was deaf
and breathless and stunned. It was not
as if the world were new and beautiful.

It was, instead, as if I had unlearned
how to use my hands
and feet. Where does the life of the body

leave off, the life of the spirit start? When
does the mouthful of air move beyond breathing
towards magic? We made

a spectacle of ourselves, dancing about
like clowns in huge shoes, goofy with happiness,
inarticulate in all but the lexicon
of sexual flesh;

and the soul, from its short-leased home
among the muscles, sent its respects,
or so we were told . . .

Even in *Paradise*, the light-filled spirits
long for their resurrection,
and Dante is surprised that they miss their bodies:

"Not only for themselves," he speculates,
"but for their mothers and fathers, and for the others
dear to them on earth,"

souls wistful for flesh, nostalgic
for their faraway, simple selves who walked about

and who, lifting and seeing their hands,
thought suddenly one day *These touch, caress, stroke*;
who found in the body a bridge beyond it

and coined the word *beloved*. And thus we performed
for ourselves the seamless changing over
of element to element,

body to air, solid to spirit, magic trick
or miracle, without knowing the particular
spell or prayer or luck that made it quicken.

GREETINGS

At six a.m., orange emerges dominant outside, corona
above gray clouds, and the first
burst of air in the door is slightly pungent:
                                        skunk,
a not-unpleasant sharpness that delineates
morning and its coolness.
A dog, unwelcome now at his owner's house,
wanders with skunk spray matted deep in his fur, a four-footed
    censer
blessing my yard, my neighbors, the road, the brightening valley.
I shiver at the threshold,
                        sniff deeply. Odor
makes the air alive: my own dogs bristle
and push past, into the dew-wet weeds and towards the river.

Dawns like this, when air
vibrates with more than the simple breeze
                                (with scent,
and longing), I wonder where they are—
the dead, I mean, whose soft movements
penetrate this still-waking world: it seems
that my father, wrapped against the damp, sets waves
of something physicists could name
careening into me,
                    a sort of greeting
fluttering in the tree—domestic, calm, and gentler
than touch. *Good morning* I think it means
(or else *good luck*), and it lends density
to a day marked with skunk-aroma
keen as the kick of reflex.
                        There's no evidence
I'm not alone, framed at the verge of the yard, welcoming no one;
but I sense a scene replete with figures—everyone
I've lost—who set the morning moving,
                                as you might

nudge the edge of a chair to watch it rock,
then slow itself and settle. The piñon
is ruffled not by wind, but by
an unignorable hand.

                Thunder curls overhead
and the downpour starts; it's the *Pastoral Symphony;*
the dogs race back from the river
spattered with mud, and grinning.
I let them in.
          I let all of them in:
my door stands open despite the rain, despite
the musk of skunks, which dissipates as I wait,
and the dead begin to fill my house as they have been doing,
    wordlessly,
as if this day were a source of calm rejoicing
too powerful for me to bear alone.

THE DOG SEASON

Mornings, the road in front of my house
trembles with runoff—last week's rains
working down from the mountains late, still in their party satins,
making for the river, one street and one field away;

and in the tiny arroyo that results, the soft clay-edged runnel,
many birds, ten or eleven, fuss at bathing. A mist
shaken from wings clouds their chattering not-yet-song
of specific pleasure.   My dog

will jump the fence these days for anything: fragrance of horse;
the mileaway yowl of a cat, or an imagined cat; he wends back
through Rivera's fields until he is decorated—
belly, paws, and ears—with seed-pods, their rasp and nap
tenacious, delicate. He sows all Nambé with new weeds, drinks
from the irrigation ditch, and finally, on Luisito's porch
with Luis in his wheelchair (as if they had been gossiping
all afternoon like two old men), politely
waits for me to come home.

Then runs with me. I bicycle along the flooded river, where
        cottonwoods
shed white tufts of the stuff they're named for
and from where the sunset is radiant with cliches . . .
Everything says *early summer, end of spring.*
The ridiculous baby goats, all bleat and stumble.
Somebody's tilled garden. Where was my own

glad rush into the season? At twilight
next to the Rio Nambé I could inhale it:
steaming mud and newborns, the yellowish
new green leaves, the dance
of canine impatience. *How often,* he asks,
must your nose be rubbed in the evidence?

Cinquains for Rocky

You want
a word that means
separating two things
by bringing them closer. "What for?"
she asks.

"Doesn't
make sense." It does,
you tell her, when one speaks
about relationships—about
you two.

Pieces for Non-Cooperative Ensemble*

for Ron Fein

I.

Imagine us separately: four
isolated figures standing out
against a darker crowd, as if lit
from inside: you and him and her
and finally me, performing an odd dance
partly partnering, partly leading on
each other, and others still unseen,
each with our own tempos, all at once
moving toward an object of desire.
One gets to the rendezvous spot late
and intercepts another, who's following
someone else, who's just gone out of sight
around a corner, exhaust clouds billowing
and hiding her—or maybe that's *her* car—

---

*The term "non-cooperative ensemble," invented by the
composer Ron Fein, indicates a group in which each
instrument plays in its own tempo, independent of the other
instruments in the ensemble.

II.

Begin again. At four starting places
in the city, A and B are leaving
work; C's cooking; D's driving
north toward A, who races
home via C's house to see
whose car's in the driveway. Meanwhile,
B calls D. No answer. Sauces boil
on C's stove: a special meal for B,
who phones ahead, "I'm running late." Crying
noiselessly, A reads a note: "I heard
about you two. I'd guessed it all along . . ."
Four principals enact together, trying,
always, to be happy with the wrong
person, the wrong timing, the wrong word.

III.

Try not to think of this as dissonance,
or as a fugue gone crazy. It's a song
made up of separate voices. Each, alone,
sounds good to you. But in this instance
we're trying a duet, and end up just
a half-step off from harmony, and don't
quite end on the same beat. Can't
you see that's not important? At the most,
it causes tension—but the music works,
if only to an educated ear.
Think of us as part of the same score
but playing independent of each other—
one sings alone awhile, the other marks
his beats of rest. But sometimes we're together.

Pastoral

I don't know much about sheep, don't know
how big they can get or how smart they are, why
they seem to come only in black and white, or how to read
the red patches of ownership blazed on their backs.
In Sligo and Donegal they crowded the car
off the road on nearly every road we drove,
with sometimes a dog or small boy chasing,
a constant glottal chatter rising from the herd.
Sheep really *do* say "baa"; they hold the breaking word
in their throats until it crumbles. It was May;
some of the lambs made their first clumsy runs
avoiding us. And hiking Slieve League
or down near Drumcliff, we found them
guarding high crosses and dolmens, grazing
the mound where a witch was buried, wandering
down to the tiny strands from their western hills;
we saw them in roofless ruins too minor
to be named in guidebooks.
                              And, on a small road,
found a diamond-shaped yellow sign with three
white sheep—a handmade "sheep crossing"
that made you laugh. When you did, I remembered
the long time it had been since I'd said
I loved you, and said it. For once
I picked a good moment: spring,
our first long time alone, and a scene
set up for lovers back in the sixteenth century.
It would have been natural for that time to be perfect—
perfect!—the definition of romance. Looking back, though,
I remember the blank faces of sheep, see
their dark ears flapping as they feed, their grave,
stupid bodies; I hear their noise.

Neons

For two weeks in the summer, she goes every morning
to water the plants at her friend's house, feed the fish,
collect the mail and the papers. Her friend
vacations in New York State, but here
the day is already hazy and full of glare, the damp
steady sort of heat that hits at dawn
and stays. The woman's glad of this little chore.
Unlocking the empty house, she listens: her heels
echo among the rooms. The fish—mostly inch-long brightnesses
called neons—dart to the floating, brittle flakes
she gives them. She turns the geraniums inward,
away from the window, and mists the fern.
The woman is calm, as if at an oasis
where her new job and odd new single life
are of no consequence; her ex-husband
will not call her here to explain again
his reasons for leaving; she will not have to learn
names of new people, or new procedures
in an unfamiliar office.

Now she passes through the other rooms
like a wing or fin, barely disturbing the air,
then locks the front door and tests to see that it's latched.
It's seven-thirty, but already her face
has a tight mask of sweat, and her blouse, gone limp,
has lost its pleats and the crisp, sweet smell of the iron.
The next day, tapping fish food into the water,
she sees on the floor to the left of the tank
a neon, dead. A slight
decaying odor reaches her: she wasn't aware,
at first, but now it seems quite strong, as if
a larger thing had died. All its orange
has faded to putty—she hates to touch it,
but scoops it up in a tissue, quickly flushes.
Then cracks a window, though there's no breeze;
heat continues to weigh on the town

like a judgment in the green shade of the street,
and it seems unlucky to start the morning with burial.

Things get worse, and next day
there's another on the floor, its gray eye
filmed with gel, and after that another.
The woman watches the tank, as if a clue
could be found in the gentle rhythms of fish,
but they seem imperturbable. When, sometimes,
she finds the house as she'd left it, the woman feels
relief, or the lifting-off of sadness, and remembers
her own unhappiness again. But three
or four times more a fish out of water
makes her wonder if there isn't, somehow, something
she doesn't know she's doing wrong. Her friend returns,
and the woman tells this story with an undertone of apology.

It seems there's an explanation. A fighting fish
she hadn't known about, that her friend had thought
was sluggish or sick, had suddenly come to life
and would sometimes chase the others
until, swimming in terror, they flipped themselves
right out of the aquarium. A simple adjustment:
the fighting fish gets moved to a tank of its own.
The woman wants to laugh with relief,
to tell her friend she thought the fish were suicides
and she somehow responsible; but now she's embarrassed
and stays quiet. Instead, she and her friend
set up the barbecue and open all the mail.
Long into the starless heavy night
they sit outside, talking in low voices, and the day's heat lifts
just slightly to a small accompaniment
of wind chimes and silverware. When it's time, the woman
walks back home alone, among the streetlamps
and isolated windows shedding light,
and what she walks through isn't the neighborhood darkness,
common enough—but the swimming thrill
of circles, the question of where to leap.

SEVEN LYRICS OF AUTUMN

Chamisa, daisies, and turning cottonwoods
are the three golds of the road-border;
asters, sky, and my bicycle the three blues;
and as for sound,
                              which in this chorus of chirp and whirr
is insect, and which the freewheel
spinning its singing chain?

Open windows.
Naked leg outside the quilt.

Cricket under the bureau
four nights.
And dogs, barking
to each other.
The loose screen
whistles, admitting

a sudden cold gust.

It's the sound of nature winding down,
                              mainsprings
of trees releasing one swift *tock* after another
toward the winterlong rest.

A tourist town, with its commerce of inn and bar,
grandeur of landscape surrounding.
Dependable (shrinking) wilderness,
boutiques for each nuance
in the *zeitgeist* . . .

and now, its sigh
heaving the last guests out.
Swept streets in brilliant slanted light.
The locals, walking,
to whom the town seems almost empty—
but familiar that way, and somehow
older, and softened.

––––––––––

Chorus of chirp and whirr:
a crowd of locusts; crickets;
                              or else
the magnified rush of blood through the body,
audible: a monstrous human purr of pleasure.
Or the mesh of gears through, more than distance,
time,
        riding in hills
under the aspened mountains, gold as of just this week.
If this racket's my doing, it's true, then,
I'm happiest as I am now:
                          alone, on a road
in a rugged landscape, headed away from home.

––––––––––

Equinox-night orchard:
apples crushed on the roadway—
delicious cool rot!

———————

One ladder with a leg gone bad; one brown bag apple-filled.
Balanced half against bough, half against three sturdy legs,
    precarious,
all morning I am the picture of industry, picking.
Neighbors offer me their trees, too,
their large peaches, their Golden Delicious,
their small, yellow plums sweet as honey—each tree
carrying more than it wants to hold
and spilling windfalls into the grass, carrying
more than even the birds will eat
and still full of fruit,
bearing, bearing.

LA BUFERA INFERNAL

We were in the subway and still friends
when the August-heavy hot rush of train
threw us off-balance. It couldn't just be wind:
it was *la bufera infernal* for you, and Dante (said
to rhyme with *shanty*, as if your prof's
Boston accent were correct), Dante
had scripted your Paolo to the wrong Francesca.
Sorry, buster, find your own gust to fly;
this *bufera*'s all mine. You're in the right place
with the wrong Italian. Try that line
on some kid who hasn't heard it—like Beatrice there
who's still in junior high, wearing a skin-tight skirt
to her Catholic school uniform, her sister's lipstick
and spike heels to die for. You could chase that lady
to hell and back and not be out of breath—
but I switch to the Number One at 59th,
and you touch my leg again, I'm calling a cop.

Paperback Romance

Everything about the girl is beautiful,
but she seems not to know it. A Heroine
should have her blind spots. She's not dependent
on parents or family. She's changing
her job, or moving. She's looking for love.
This is the biggest moment in her life.

She's got clear skin, no weight problem, social life
full of dates, a good wardrobe, beautiful
bone structure, the works. Everything but Love,
in short, without which she's no Heroine.
Enter the Hero, not married but changing
his mind about it, decision dependent

on available prospects—dependent
on all the old values. Until now, life
has been easy: he's ready for changing
into a family man, with beautiful
kids, a wife, a station wagon. Our Heroine
steps into the picture. It's instant love.

The trouble is, she can't believe it's Love.
She thinks it's a crush. She's not independent
enough to tell him that real Heroines
always get their men. And this *is* real life,
isn't it? He's dating, too, a beautiful
Other Woman so classy she's changing

her clothes every other page, and changing
the Hero's feelings with them. *Is this love?*
he asks himself. *Sure, she may be beautiful,*
sophisticated and all, dependent
on my sensitive strength, but isn't life
more than being virile? Well, the Heroine

has run off by herself, as Heroines
sometimes do, and now she's bent on changing

her goody-two-shoes image, seeing life's
too short, et cetera. She wins the love
of the Hero in a scene dependent
on suspension of disbelief. Beautiful

wedding, The End. The Heroine says love
in this changing world is completely dependent
on staying beautiful, leading a virtuous life.

A LOVE SONG FROM THE CHIMAYÓ LANDFILL

You'd have liked everything about this,
the brilliant sky hard as a jewel, and the kids
providing a sort of irresponsible background music,
entirely appropriate, and the aluminum-can collectors
smiling, with their bounty stacked by their pickup.
Even the dogs were smiling, wagging and sniffing
by the dead animal pit (whose stolen sign
turned up at a girls' dorm in Albuquerque);
and maybe one of these dogs will gleefully roll
in an old carcass, as wolves do,
and as your dog did once, and had to be brought home
walking mournfully behind the car. I had merely
two bags of garbage to heave into the heap,
a minor offering beside that of the men
emptying their truckbeds with shovels. They
were happy, too; yes, everyone was laughing,
as if it were Fiesta, not the dump. I wanted to tell you:
this is how you make me feel, my darling.

Tarantulas, in Autumn, Seek Their Mates

In the October forest
we did not care about
chiaroscuro—
nearly transparent blonde aspens
among their sponsoring pines,
the shadow-striped wind. We kept
our eyes on the road edge
until *There's one*
Bill said. The tarantula

elegant in motion: old man
waltzing a bride: dignity
and each foot
where it ought to go.
Six in an hour
crossed that pavement, and took
summer with them,
away from us, into the warm earth.

AVIARY

Like flags in the plowed soil, or sprouts
of bird: fifty-some standing egrets
waiting, looking. From the car we saw
their rise and veer. You said, "Oaxaca."

We headed there, where already
peacocks and cockatoos, crying, spread
their million hues in one blue blur; macaws
taught *Buenos Días* to the chained parrot.
Others—the mynah, toucans, ducks
clipped and swimming, and migrant flocks
in transit, like the egrets, studded
the tourist garden. The white legions added
some foreign mystery: their loose veil
of beaks and wings dipped to the pool
as if flung by a dancer; they ascended again
in a single arc.
               The cloud of them swam
above the *zocalo.* There, pigeons
hung to the stone facade that hid them
in saints' gray robes: why
these clung to the cathedral, or what *sky*
meant to the gaudy others, whose wings
were crippled beyond all flying,
were questions better unasked. In flight
ourselves, we risk our own straight
routes to winds and customs, risk lift
and questions: yet the tropical calls
from the garden, *Oaxaca,* were almost inaudible
or, *Oaxaca,* unbearably shrill.

Manzanillo

Manzanillo. She says it perfectly,
like something off a menu, easily
as *margarita, cerveza.* The rim
of this beach, a tourist's brochure-fed dream
of sand and exotica, is as tame
to her as her childhood Florida home;
here, again, she flourishes in the sun.
Near her, two photographers have begun
shooting a fashion layout: models drift
sullenly to the water, bright clothes left
in a trail behind. To their right, a man
makes time with the girl selling hydroplane
tickets. A windsurfer's gold sail sinks down.
Some stand in the water; others have gone
walking in town. Nobody speaks Spanish
here, as if the whole place needed practice
in other languages.
                                    But she is strong
in the private dialects of longing:
all this time she's felt close to women known
only for minutes, from far off. Alone,
she watched peasants in the city, the plain
women who crawled on their knees to the shrine
of the Virgin, or beggars in the grid
of buildings, taxis, buildings, and noise. Spreading
blankets in a *mercado,* dark women
worked the dark stalls of weavings: but the men,
buying, bargained their prices to nothing.
What could she do but watch, stiffly nodding
"Yes, yes, let's go"? In a farm-green village
between the volcanoes, a girl's usage
of *necesario* taught her it meant
outhouse; later, she knew she overspent,
paying a child's asking price for carvings
of rabbits in alabaster. Leaving
those women, those villages, for this beach,
she made a trade, taking—Beauty for Truth?

Or was it the vigorous Pacific
for real lives? Here, professionals pose, slick
with oil, their bored and practiced faces tricked
to mimic seduction; after the shoot
they slink to the hidden beach to swim nude
in black water. She's practically asleep
in sand as cozy as a lover's lap;
when she does look, the sun is much too bright
to disclose an undeformed beach: no, it
is dappled with figments, the waves are still
at a quiet shore, and nothing is real.

Nocturne in a Western Landscape

How plain it looks from bed,
out the window: the night
a coat you slip into before holding me,

the simple moon full
and wearing her one lace.

Past the invisible valley a spine
of lights marks a trail:
it's the only road out.

By day the land is a bled-dry color
whose silver-green, you tell me,

mocks botany. Trees
from our old life zoom back to us
like Disney, wide-screened:

in the happy ending, hills
are covered with broad strokes

of proper emerald, not pieced
like a first quilt,
from a spectrum of drabs;

not littered with junipers
random as scattered buttons.

These fields are straw, this sky
pearl gray—colors of garments
faded from overuse,

yet new somehow. When it's dark
like this, we stop our running;

if the plain night beckons regardless,
its pattern of stars
is no lit route. In moonlight

our own dim shapes are
blunt and familiar: all we recognize.

THE MIRACLE AS I SEE IT

Believe it, they said:
   you won't be able to drive for them all,
they flank both sides of the road, and they walk
      slowly, as if they couldn't get run over
on their way to Mass. I didn't think
      the world still harbored pilgrims, who'd
show up on this two-lane road in their jogging suits
      carrying staves, carrying crosses,
whole families with children running ahead,
      old people again making the trip they vowed
x number of years ago to make each Lent
      as part of a bargain with God: I didn't think it,
but so it was. At Chimayó, a wall
      is shingled with crutches, and adobe
shelters the healing soil
      from which the miracles fly. Take
a pinch of dust under your tongue, rub some
      on an ulcer—once, I saw someone
snort a portion—then wait
      while the miracle brews to full potency:
and this possibility, this imminence, draws
      bureaucrats from their sad Capitol offices,
technicians from Los Alamos and the common
      factual answers; this
draws them on foot eight miles, eleven, twenty-five,
      and those from Albuquerque walk
almost a hundred. All of them pass my house.

In Española the paper reports one sighting
      of the Devil at Saints and Sinners Bar;
another at the Line Camp; another
      on the road to Peñasco, where, hitching,
he turned down a ride in a pickup
      because the driver's name was Juan. At the bar,
a woman said he was dressed in white,
      quite dapper, and had long nails,
but she didn't know until she kissed him

that he wasn't human. An onlooker guessed
the Devil had a hard time here in the Valley—
    it's not Santa Fe, he said, where Satan's
got everyone already.
    At work, no one believes these stories.
They're glad there's no worse news
    for the paper to print; it reminds them
of when the woman making enchiladas
    saw the face of Christ in a tortilla
and straightaway set up a shrine. There are miracles
    and then miracles; thus everyone still asks
one another, *Will you be walking this year?*
    Oh, the answer comes, *I always walk.*

On Good Friday some of the stores close up
    and people take the day off,
parking their cars off Highway 4 in Pojoaque
    early, before it gets hot. Many
think this pilgrimage will help them, even
    if they doubt that dirt from the Sanctuario
actually cures the lame, much less that Christ
    ever reveals himself in a round of bread;
there's a logic to these things in which
    the show of faith—any at all—is the gesture,
regardless of reward. Over coffee I watch
    the morning parade of souls. It is
the miracle as I see it:
    nineteen ninety-one, and a crowd
votes with its feet for the resurrection,
    a heaven of saints, and answers to prayer,
for healing, for sacred earth. If this can be,
    couldn't what's here on the sidelines
be wondrous too: Catalino burning trash,
    me with my cup, someone
retrieving a morning paper? — Not contradictions,
    but people with other means
to what ends for some in Chimayó, new ways
    next to the old, a remarkable dailiness,

one foot after the other, treading
    calloused parts of ourselves that represent
how difficult it is to believe, to live
    by what we believe, to show whatever we believe in
that we are coming,
    are already on our way.

Notes on the Poems

The pilgrimage referred to in "The Miracle as I See It" is the Good Friday pilgrimage to the Sanctuario de Chimayó in Chimayó, New Mexico. Chimayó, Nambé, Española, Peñasco, and Pojoaque (pronounced poh-WAH-kay) are all communities in Northern New Mexico.

In "Aviary": Oaxaca is pronounced wah-HAH-kah.

In *"La Bufera Infernal,"* the reference to Dante is from *Inferno* V.

In *"The Love of the Flesh,"* the reference to Dante is from *Paradiso XIV.*

Acknowledgements

Grateful acknowledgement is made to the following publications, in which some of these poems have appeared (sometimes in different form):

The Agni Review: "Charleston," *Antaeus*: "Aviary," *The Fireweed Journal*: "Nocturne in a Western Landscape," "Tarantulas, in Autumn, Seek Their Mates," *Hayden's Ferry Review*: "*Chez Persephone*," "Hibiscus," *New Letters*: "Pieces for Non-Cooperative Ensemble," *Poetry Northwest*: "The Dog Season," *Prairie Schooner*: "Seven Lyrics of Autumn," *Shenandoah*: "Neons," *Shock's Bridge*: "Tall Dark Man Asleep on a Bench," and *Tar River Poetry*: "Love of the Flesh."

"Aviary," "Charleston," "Cinquains for Rocky," "*La Bufera Infernal*," "Muscle Memory," "Other Longevities," "Paperback Romance," and "Pastoral" appeared in a chapbook, *Paperback Romance*, published by State Street Press (1984).

"Aviary" was reprinted in *The State Street Reader*, edited by Judith Kitchen (State Street Press, 1990) and in *The Anthology of Magazine Verse and Yearbook of American Poetry 1985*.

"A Love Song from the Chimayó Landfill" appeared in *National Poetry Competition Winners 1991*, published by the Chester H. Jones Foundation.

"Pastoral" was reprinted in *The Forgotten Language*, edited by Christopher Merrill (Peregrine Smith Books, 1991).

Thanks to the Corporation of Yaddo and the MacDowell Colony for the time and space in which to write some of the poems included in this book, and to the Minnesota State Arts Board for its support. For their encouragement and patience, my appreciation to Charles Bell, Gloria Brame, Harriet Cole, Bill Cross, Bob Douglass, Barry Fogden, Al Greenberg, Akua Lezli Hope, Jean Kilczer, Thomas Lux, Heather McHugh, Susan Methvin, David Mutschlecner, David Nolf, Scott Serkes, Gregory Blake Smith, Marcia Southwick, and Ellen Bryant Voigt.

About the Author

Janet Holmes is the author of *Paperback Romance* (State Street Press, 1984) and recipient of a Minnesota State Arts Board grant and a Bush Foundation Artist's Fellowship. Her poems have been published in numerous magazines, including *Antaeus, New Letters, Poetry Northwest, Prairie Schooner, Puerto del Sol, Shenandoah,* and *Tar River Poetry.* A longtime resident of New Mexico, she now lives in Minnesota with her husband, Alvin Greenberg, and Wally, Waverly, and Daisy.

ANHINGA PRIZE FOR POETRY

Selection: Judge:

Janet Holmes   1993
The Physicist at the Mall   Joy Harjo

Earl S. Braggs   1992
Hat Dancer Blue   Marvin Bell

Jean Monahan   1991
Hands   Donald Hall

(no winner)   1990
                                            Denise Levertov

Nick Bozanic   1989
The Long Drive Home   Judith Hemschemeyer

Julianne Seeman   1988
Enough Light to See   Charles Wright

Will Wells   1987
Conversing with the Light   Henry Taylor

Robert Levy   1986
The Whistle Maker   Robin Skelton

Judith Kitchen   1985
Perennials   Hayden Carruth

Sherry Rind   1984
The Hawk in the Back Yard   Louis Simpson

Ricardo Pau-Llosa   1983
Sorting Metaphors   William Stafford

OTHER BOOKS FROM ANHINGA PRESS

P.V. LeForge   *The Secret Life of Moles*

Gary Corseri   *Random Descent*

Michael Mott   *Counting the Grasses*

Yvonne Sapia   *The Fertile Crescent*

Rick Lott   *Digging for Shark Teeth*

Ryals and Decker, eds.   *North of Wakulla:*
                               An Anhinga Anthology

Jordan and Shows, eds.   *Cafe at St. Marks:*
                               The Apalachee Poets